I0357680

Warning Signs of the Huli Jings

© **JENNIFER TRUONG**, 2021

ISBN 9781648411069

This is Microcosm #687

This edition © Microcosm Publishing, 2018-2020

For a catalog, write or visit:

Microcosm Publishing

2752 N Williams Ave.

Portland, OR 97227

www.Microcosm.Pub

To join the ranks of high-class stores that feature Microcosm titles, talk to your rep: In the U.S. **Como** (Atlantic), **Fujii** (Midwest), **Book Travelers West** (Pacific), **Turnaround** in Europe, **Manda/UTP** in Canada, **New South** in Australia, and **GPS** in Asia, India, Africa, and South America. We are sold in the gift market by **Gifts of Nature** and **Faire.**

Did you know that you can buy our books directly from us at sliding scale rates? Support a small, independent publisher and pay less than Amazon's price at www.**Microcosm.Pub**

Global labor conditions are bad, and our roots in industrial Cleveland in the 70s and 80s made us appreciate the need to treat workers right. Therefore, our books are MADE IN THE USA and printed on post-consumer paper.

Microcosm Publishing is Portland's most diversified publishing house and distributor with a focus on the colorful, authentic, and empowering. Our books and zines have put your power in your hands since 1996, equipping readers to make positive changes in their lives and in the world around them. Microcosm emphasizes skill-building, showing hidden histories, and fostering creativity through challenging conventional publishing wisdom with books and bookettes about DIY skills, food, bicycling, gender, self-care, and social justice. What was once a distro and record label was started by Joe Biel in his bedroom and has become among the oldest independent publishing houses in Portland, OR. We are a politically moderate, centrist publisher in a world that has inched to the right for the past 80 years.

The Warning Signs of Huli Jings

Warning & Disclaimer

This publication may be sensitive for some but is for educational purposes only and is not intended to be a substitute for professional mental health advice, diagnosis, or treatment. Do not disregard professional mental health advice or delay seeking it based by the following. If you feel distraught, please see provided resources in the back pages of this zine.

Preface

The year of 2020 has been far from perfect. As countless national and global injustices continue over a novel pandemic, the current state of the world may feel well beyond overwhelming. We may not have immediate answers to all political or social problems and not all situations are controllable, but we can always start from within and foster our personal lives. With proper identification of problems, specific precautions can be taken to avoid them. This publication shares insight on how to recognize and prepare oneself from potential harms aggravated by toxic behavior.

There is now a familiarity with the insidious nature of COVID-19, but toxic behavior, also uneasily detected with the naked eye, has become rampant, normalized, and even accepted. Like learning about the new disease, the details of the virus weren't widely known and understood at first, but we learn to cope better through recognizing what is harmful. As we continue to inspect the values of life, there is a necessity and urgency to acknowledge toxic behavior because it provokes a dark reality, perpetuates negativity, and produces a hurt society.

This publication is dedicated towards identifying manipulation, dehumanization, and abuse. It brings practical solutions as to not fall victim to dangerous patterns and how to defuse them in times of interpersonal conflicts. The author hopes to inspire speaking up against the suffering of others and oneself. With much love, this zine is created for you or someone you know.

狐狸精

KITSUNE

キツネ

HỒ LY TINH

구미호

KUMIHO

Huli Jing
Fox Spirit

The name "Huli Jing" translates to "fox spirit" in Chinese. It originates from China but appears as adaptations in other East Asian folklores, literatures, and mythologies. "Huli Jings" are often depicted in stories as mischievous, shapeshifting, deceitful, creatures disguised as humans. Though they are mostly illustrated as female characters rather than male, gender has no effect describing their toxic activities. They commonly serve as the antagonists of cautionary tales using devious techniques and conniving schemes.

The following passages will explore several criteria and traits of Huli Jings and how to look for, avoid, manage, or keep peace with them. However, they have varying degrees of deception, questionable morals, and desires as not all Huli Jings are the same. What makes one a Huli Jing manifest in form is that in most cases, their pathological urges are not isolated events. The characteristics of Huli Jings encompass the subsequent personalities with descriptors from western psychology; further defined in the glossary.

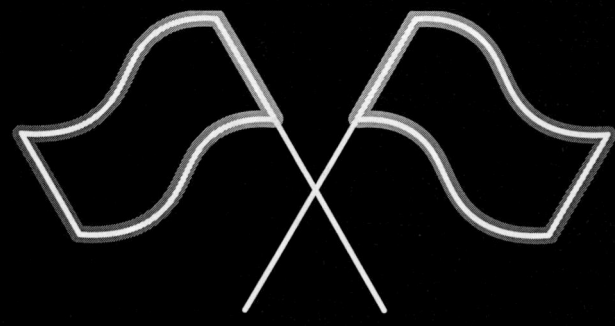

Narcissism

Note that not all narcissists are Huli Jings, but all Huli Jings contain self-centered attributes. Although narcissism exist on an extensive spectrum, it is the very foundation of what Huli Jings are built on. According to the Diagnostic and Statistical Manual of Mental Disorders (DSM), someone with narcissistic personality disorder (NPD) is different from someone with narcissistic qualities. There are many other types such as the classic grandiose, the vulnerable, and malignant. Then there are subtypes such overt and covert. The following will specifically cover the latter and focus on covert narcissism since it is generally less obvious and deserves more coverage to gain awareness.

While self-esteem is necessary for one's happiness it becomes destructive when one's confidence becomes toxically grandiose. It is healthy to have a positive amount of self-image, but it can get out of hand when a person over relies on bolstering themselves and putting down others as the main way of relating to the world. It doesn't allow room to be challenged and learn from challenged experiences.

People who are Huli Jings have inflated egos and a strong sense of entitlement. Figuratively, they ride on high horses and without warrant press their victims to prove themselves. They flaunt superiority over others by belittling other people's issues and even successes. Unfortunately, this major feature deters them from any true self-reflection and aids dishonest personalities to continue. Thinking anything could be wrong is not an idea they enjoy or fathom, but consequential symptoms do not go unseen.

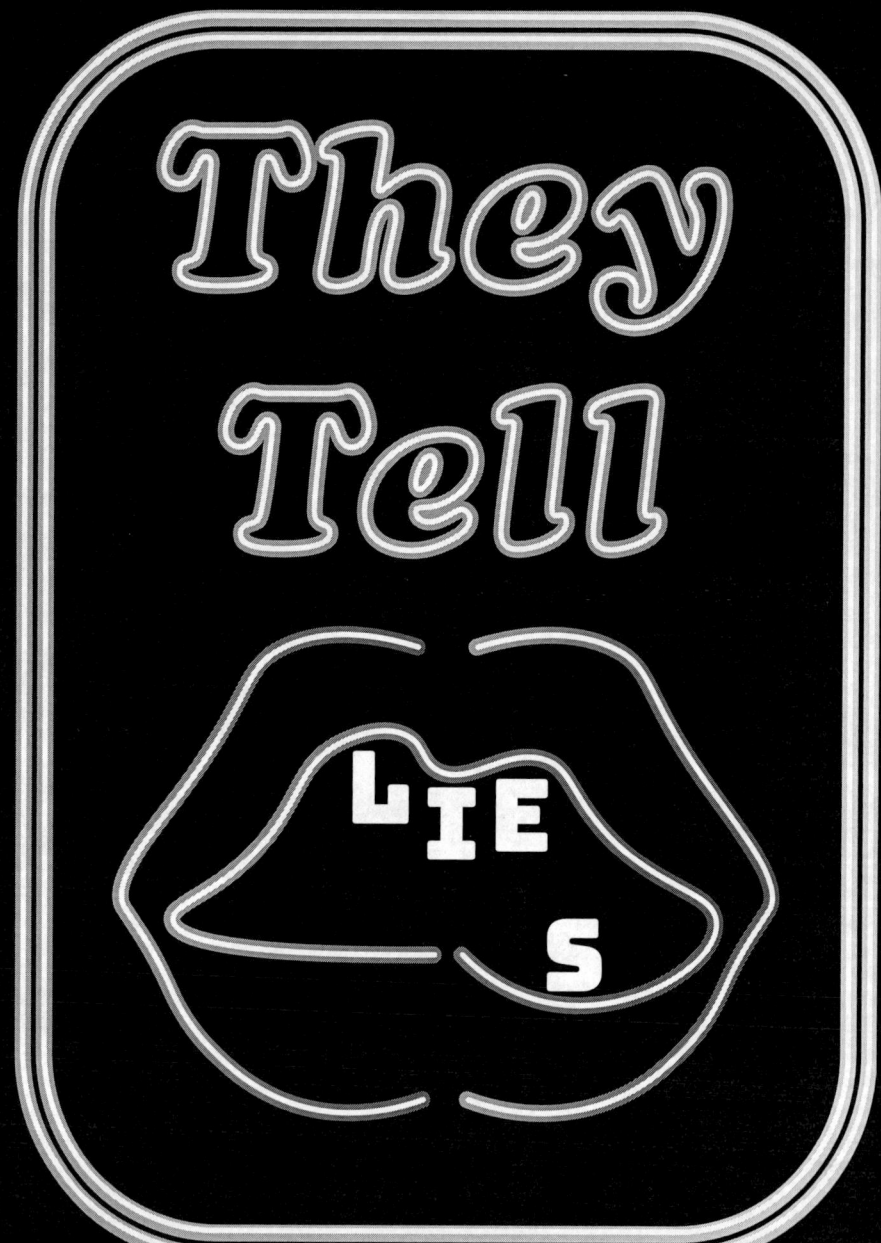

Lying

To gain a better understanding of Huli Jings, we must understand first and foremost that they habitually lie. Anything they say, good or bad, can be misrepresentations when it suits their favor or self-image. Huli Jings are masters at manipulation. It is unclear whether the perpetrators may or may not be aware of their lack of inner value and integrity, therefore they manipulate others, and they don't hesitate to unethically exploit opportunities when they feasibly arise.

Rarely do Huli Jings take ownership of their perverse actions because they project faults onto others. Huli Jings have a great incompetence to self-govern. With everything to gain by making others look bad, they fail to admit their own faults and accuse victims of possessing them. It is a common defense mechanism. Defenses are natural, but projection is primitive and confusing. Huli Jings are motivated to spin details against individuals and reject being held accountable. If and when they do take accountability, their justifications are rather superficial and lack genuine remorse as their life's story is about the unforgiving manipulation of others to maintain their grander narrative.

power control issues

flaws

self-absorbed

RUDE

Triangulator

They portray themselves as innocent victims, but in actuality they render themselves as the undisclosed triangulator. They break friends and families apart by setting people up against each other and create psychological warfare. They twist words, spread misinformation, and deliberately depict their victims under false premises. They are the most powerful when they are able to isolate their prey to gain power. This side of themselves is not revealed in group settings. Triangulated spaces are created by the puppet masters to foster mistrust, so they govern in the chaotic dynamic of others. Huli Jings triangulate because they crave attention, validation, and power to control. They revel in the madness.

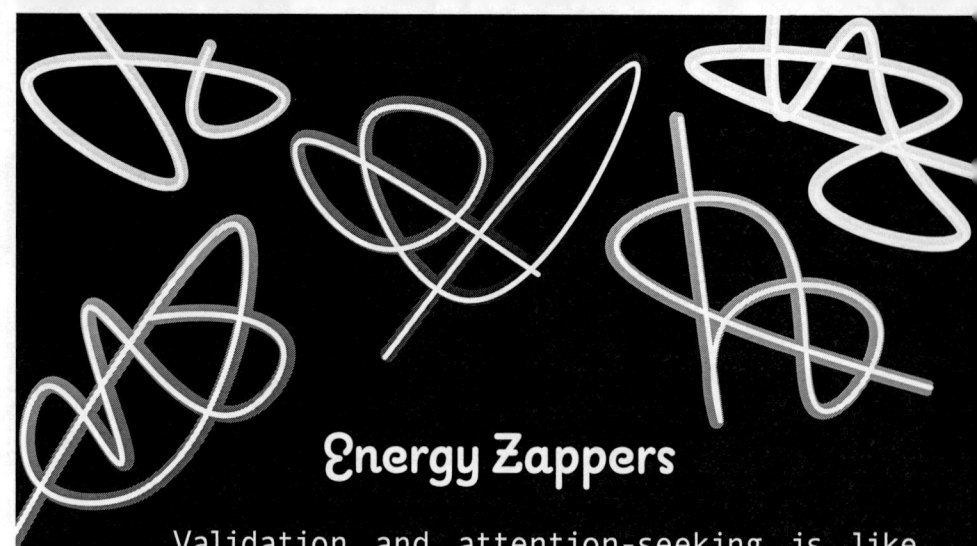

Energy Zappers

Validation and attention-seeking is like food to a Huli Jing. It fuels their ego. They have a rigid view of what they want their validation to be. Any validation not what they want the validation to be will starve a Huli Jing's survival. If confronted with the criticism, it ceases their supply. Specific search for validation is known as narcissistic supply. Narcissistic supply can come from people, things, or objects that superficially authenticates the Huli Jing's need to be admired. It helps guard their vulnerable sense of self because they get endorsed by the general public.

DO NOT FEED

They Blow Up

A major red flag in how to distinguish a Huli Jing is recognizing immature behavior. Consistent immaturity are displays of stunted emotional growth. It becomes a clear admonition when they are acting like a petty tyrant or spoiled child trying to take toll on the reactions of others. They get frazzled and hostile over hairline triggers that established adults wouldn't typically get upset about, and they expect preferential treatment. If that is not received, they can become demanding, punishing, and explosive. This is also known as adult tantrums. While there are acceptable responses to anger such as crying and being distraught, acting out like an uncaring demon is not. Integrating feedback is not something Huli Jings react well to. They're a vile delinquent when triggered. When their fragile egos are injured, these fits can be seen as terrifying, ridiculous, and perhaps trivial.

On one hand...

At worst, Huli Jings resort to physical violence such as hitting, pushing, breaking and throwing things. Huli Jings can respond to criticism with intense rage and negativity. This would stop anyone from further intervening. The burst of anger is meant to intimidate and frighten victims into obedience. They don't reason with evidence or facts, but only focus their need to be right.

...they'll act out

And the other...

At best, Huli Jings express their discrepancies through being passive aggressive. It means that they will indirectly try to get a message across without attempting proper and civil communication but rather by inducing injurious mood states. Sometimes this is demonstrated in their harsh choice of words in arguments, or in punishing actions to get even. They violate conventional social boundaries and behave just like a bully. Gratitude is rarely seen in their attitudes.

... they'll act out

Gaslighting

Another type of diversion Huli Jings use in confrontations to deflect any wrongdoings are referred to as gaslighting. It is a circular system that takes over the forefront of the Huli Jing's attention to manipulate and brainwash the victim's perception of reality. This can occur in forms of verbal, emotional, or physical hostility used to confuse, defeat, or dominate. They do this by eroding what someone believes, thinks, and feels, turning worlds upside down. Gaslighting is not a normal or rational discussion and the Huli Jing defensiveness is on, fight or flight, survival mode. Other ways of gaslighting comes through minimizing, withholding, or contradicting the other person.

Gaslighting may sound like the other person exclaiming, "I didn't say that!" when you know they have had if not strongly implying so. It's purpose is to make a victim question their reality. Another example would sound like, "Why are you still talking to me if I'm a liar?". Their remarks are far from helpful or constructive in any conversations to clear air or gain clarity.

Not falling victim is about trusting your intuition and validating yourself without their approval. Otherwise, the victim will spiral into falsely created self-doubts. Before engaging with their attacks, be confident and know your facts before stepping into their traps. Hold space for yourself when they do not.

Compassion

Regrettably, Huli Jings prey on the most self-doubting, sensitive, and trusting people. If the victim's integrity, personality, wellbeing, and security depend on what others think, it makes a victim extremely susceptible to narcissistic abuse. They make easy targets for Huli Jings to feed off their low self-esteem. Even those who have a good sense of themselves are less susceptible to psychological abuse, however it does not make them immune. Huli Jings persist in their coercion, and their negative dynamics can wear down solid individuals over time, too. Abuse isn't always obvious, but the most silent ones, emotional or verbal, are just as harmful as physical.

Any relationships with a Huli Jing are clearly not sympathetic, mindful, or sane. They are not only caustic to others but also to themselves. The chances of Huli Jings having real friendships are basically none because they're unable to sustain them for long. Their idea of reality is so skewed that everyone around them are cruel and deceitful, masking and ignoring the Huli Jing's own actions. Huli Jings do not adopt healthy coping mechanisms and learn loving, nourishing behaviors. They are likely faced with unresolved issues and turn to disparaging outlets that simultaneously reflect and further spread the state of their internal mayhem.

HURT PEOPLE SOMETIMES

SOMETIMES HURT PEOPLE

Stop Causing Harm

Problem Solving

Huli Jings true objectives are not the sufferer's burden to decipher nor mend. We can't change Huli Jings who don't have the capacity of having decent character. Sometimes their toxic behaviors are more than just fleeting temperament flaws. It is often futile to call Huli Jings out because they might simply not have the resources, insight, or willingness to change, but know the problem is not the victims. While people do change, it is unwise to expect Huli Jings to change. Life itself continues to move on even when they don't and investing anymore time only enables them. Saying no is the only way to go.

People with unsettling manners are dealing with insecurities themselves. They are likely self-loathers evading their true selves manifested by their need to use others. Their behavior can be influenced by everything from upbringing, early history, environment, and even genetics. We may never truly know, but the best way out of their web of entanglement is to minimize expectations, keep a healthy distance, hold your ground, know your worth, and leave. It is best to cease contact, not engaging, not explaining, not personalizing, and step away to free ourselves. It is only a matter of time until Huli Jings can no longer pretend to regulate their emotions, hide allegations resulted from their actions, and be found out. Don't feel bad for who hurts you.

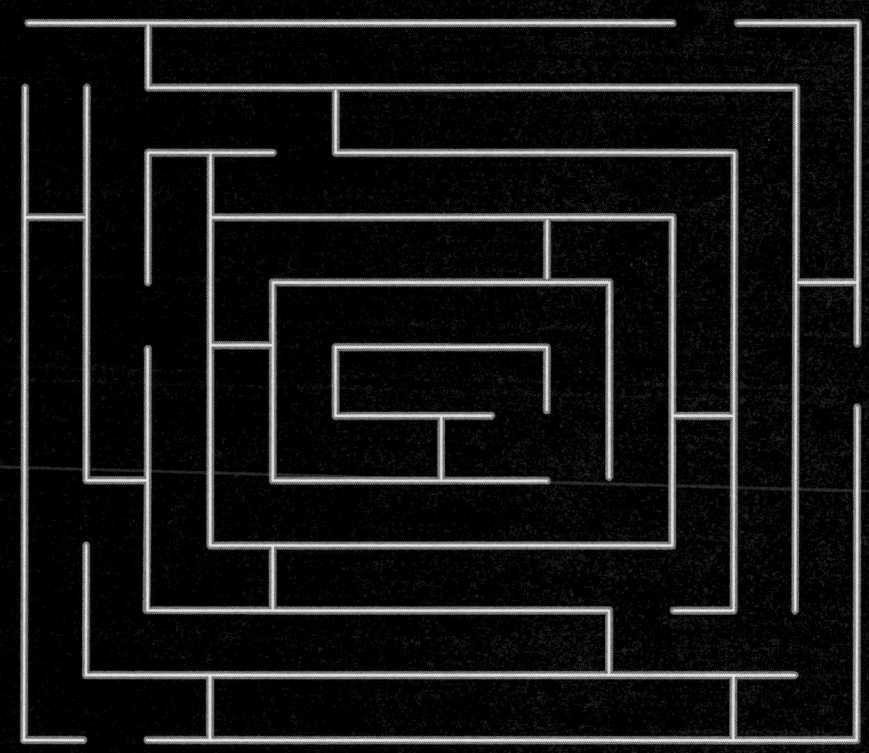

Show Yourself Love

While it is important to have kindness and understanding where a disturbed mind is coming from, while the contributing factors are not untrue, people are responsible for their own engagements and feelings about them. To personally unwind and upheave themselves from causing more harm is work they need to do. We can healthily exercise the state of consciousness we allow ourselves to exist in and not make excuses for poor behavior. It is encouraged to cease associating with them. If you feel unsafe to cut ties with a Huli Jing, talk to someone in a position of authority, mental health professional, or legal advisor.

It is of great importance to keep an open line of communication with close friends and family about Huli Jings course of actions when uncertain. The people who protect us can often help validate or explain them. By acknowledging what the Huli Jing is doing, you have taken away their power to hurt you and gain the power to look after yourself and create joy.

If you recognize and are reflective of conducts in this text, it should not be a source of shame so much as a wakeup call. This is a chance to become a better person, to fix the interpersonal problems in your life, and even repair broken relationships. We all respond to trauma differently and the way of expressions we use also vary. Most people don't always know how to communicate in constructive ways, but gaining awareness is a step in the right direction. Self-awareness is key and self-awareness can grow. The world may be unfair but to strive to live in a just one, moral responsibilities must apply to us all. We each need to do our share of deep dive into our own psyche to learn about our strengths and vulnerabilities.

HEALING

BOUNDARIES

TOXICITY

Conclusion

A widespread outbreak during the 21st century is just one more of the many unknowns we are learning about as we go. As time progresses, old information gets replaced with new data. Expanding our depths of understanding has no end. The author recognizes the subject of toxicity will change and develop for the better as more light and respect shines onto the abyss of mental and spiritual wellness. So, the reader of this zine should always continue their search for truth.

Research and acceptance have helped civilization prosper. We are not aware of something until we are made aware of it. That's how research has allowed us to be aware of the pandemic and likewise aware of toxic personality traits. Through this awareness, we learn to accept and how to process. Through study and self-realization, may we each do our part to take our fate up a notch. The age of humanity is merely just a sliver, but history has shown us how to evolve. We should always aspire to do our part better than before.

Postscript

There are resources to help with exhausted emotions. Everyone deserves the help they need, but it starts with helping ourselves first. It is crucial to seek help after any physically or mentally traumatic event. What is left unaddressed will haunt us and manifest as inflicting and repeating hurtful behaviors despite good intentions.

After experiencing the toxic behaviors of Huli Jings, it is critical to work on the necessary healing. Whether we are affected by Huli Jings or are becoming one ourselves. They do not go away on their own, and unsuspectingly feed the progression of Huli Jing traits, creating more inauspicious cycles of life.

Prolonged distress affects both the mind and body as they tend to escalate. Potential physical health impairments can look like under- or over-eating, bodily inflammations, and substance abuse. It can wear the body down and let it become more susceptible to a weakened immune system which may lead to a number of ailments and somatic diseases. To avoid these complications, it is vital to seek help sooner than later. Do not ignore any signs of unclear emotions which can set one back from experiencing life at its best. While any situation can be worse, it can also be better. If you need mental health counseling, please contact your primary care provider, student counseling, health center, or your county crisis hotline.

Glossary

ABUSE is to hurt or injure by maltreatment; ill-use.

ADULT TANTRUM is a violent demonstration of rage or frustration; a sudden burst of ill temper acted out by an adult rather than a child.

BOUNDARIES are the limits of one's personal space, including physical, psychosocial, and interpersonal domains.

BULLYING is to treat in an overbearing or intimidating manner.

COVERT NARCISSISM is the opposite of overt narcissism where the narcissistic qualities are less obvious and even purposely well-hidden.

GASLIGHTING is a form of psychological manipulation in which a person or a group covertly sows seeds of doubt in a targeted individual or group, making them question their own memory, perception, or judgment.

NARCISSISM is the pursuit of gratification from vanity or egotistic admiration of one's idealized self-image and attributes.

MANIPULATION is to change by artful or unfair means so as to serve one's purpose.

NARCISSISM is the pursuit of gratification from vanity or egotistic admiration of one's idealized self-image and attributes.

NARCISSISTIC PERSONALITY DISORDER (NPD) is a personality disorder characterized by a long-term pattern of exaggerated feelings of self-importance, an excessive craving for admiration, and struggles with empathy.

NARCISSISTIC SUPPLY is a psychological concept which describes a type of admiration, interpersonal support or sustenance drawn by an individual from his or her environment.

OVERT NARCISSISM is the most obvious form of narcissism where the narcissistic qualities are arrogant, boastful and demanding.

PASSIVE AGGRESSION is being, marked by, or displaying behavior characterized by the expression of negative feelings, resentment, and aggression in an unassertive passive way.

PHYSICAL ABUSE is any act resulting in a nonaccidental physical injury, including not only intentional assault but also the results of unreasonable punishment.

PROJECTION is the attribution of one's own attitudes, feelings, or suppositions to others, thought in psychoanalytic theory to be an unconscious defense against anxiety or guilt.

TRIANGULATION is when one person seeks to control a three-person interpersonal situation for their own benefit. It often involves the use of threats of exclusion or strategies that aim to divide and conquer.

VERBAL ABUSE is harsh and insulting language directed at a person.

JENN is True Wrong, a designer and visual artist. She is dedicated to producing projects by sharing learned contents through creativity.

Email: hello@truewrong.com
Instagram: @true.wrong

Microcosm's First Edition (100 copies), May 2021
Published by True Wrong
www.truewrong.com
Artwork, Layout, Words, Design: JENN
Printed: Microcosm Publishing

ALL WORKS © 2021 by True Wrong.
All Rights Reserved.

No portion of the publication may be reproduced or transmitted in any form or by any means without permission, except for the case of reviews.

SPECIAL THANKS:

Julie Duong
John Schwarz
Denny Katz
Olive Kimoto
Matthew Donovan

& every friend who has shown support throughout this publishing!

More health building blocks at www.Microcosm.Pub

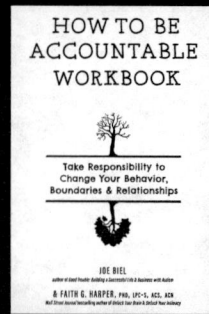

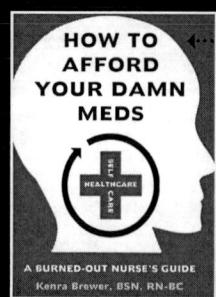

SUBSCRIBE!

For as little as $15/month, you can support a small, independent publisher and get every book that we publish—delivered to your doorstep!

www.Microcosm.Pub/BFF

Reach Out

Emergency: 911

National Domestic Violence Hotline:
1- 800-799-7233

National Hopeline Network:
1-800-SUICIDE (800-784-2433)

Crisis Text Line:
Text "HOME" TO 741-741

www.stopbullying.gov
www.crisistextline.org
www.betterhelp.com

Website

Sources